T4-AJU-233

Sapphires

Are a Girl's Best Friend

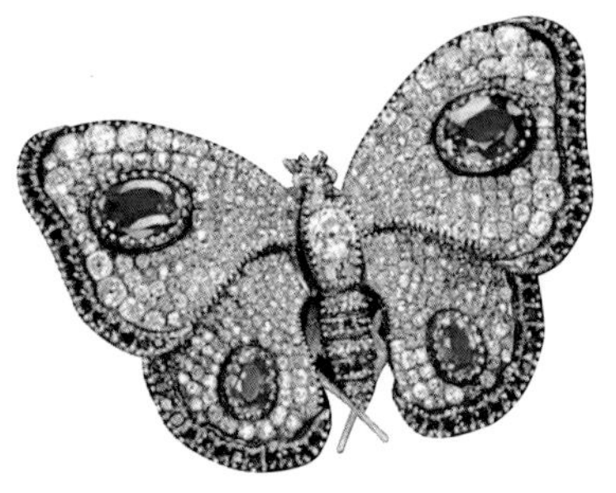

Sapphires
Are a Girl's Best Friend

SUE HEADY

Introduction by
Michael O'Donoghue

CHARTWELL
BOOKS, INC.

This edition published in 1999 by
CHARTWELL BOOKS, INC.
A division of BOOK SALES, INC
114 Northfield Avenue,
Edison, New Jersey 08837

Produced by
PRC Publishing Ltd,
Kiln House, 210 New Kings Road,
London SW6 4NZ

ISBN 0 78581 100 1

Printed and bound in Hong Kong

Contents

INTRODUCTION

Sapphires can be any color except red — red ones are called rubies, but both stones are varieties of the mineral corundum. To obtain blue sapphire, both iron and titanium need to be present when the crystal is growing and, as these elements are more common than chromium (which gives the red in ruby), blue sapphires are more easily found than rubies. Blue is the most desirable color in sapphires, but opinions differ as to which type of blue is the most beautiful. Myanmar, already famous for the world's finest rubies, also produces the finest blue sapphires: they are a deep royal blue but not so deep as to appear black by reflected light. Sapphires from Sri Lanka, where the stones occur in gem gravel rather than in hard rock, are a softer, lighter blue, while stones from other parts of southeast Asia, Thailand, and Kampuchea are a darker blue, but less deep than Myanmar stones. Australian sapphires are the characteristic dark blue, nearly black, stones.

Many connoisseurs hold Kashmir sapphires to be even finer than Myanmar ones: the mines, at an altitude which allows working to take place during only a small part of the year, produce material only sporadically; but both Myanmar and Kashmir stones achieve locality citations in salesroom catalog entries. Both Myanmar and Sri Lanka also produce fine star sapphires in which a six-rayed star can be seen at the top of the dome-shaped,

UCTION

flat-backed cabochon. As with the star ruby, a combination of fine color with a sharp, well-centered star will fetch the highest prices.

It is possible to lighten the color of large, dark blue stones by careful heating — the inclusions, which can tell the gemmologist where the stone came from, do not disappear. It is therefore possible to say that a particular specimen is from Myanmar, Sri Lanka, Thailand, or Australia. It is harder to identify sapphires whose internal fractures have been filled with polymer or glassy material, and with important sapphires, like rubies and emeralds, every effort

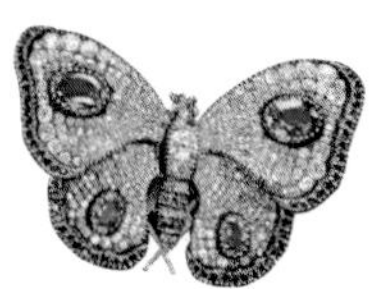

must be made to identify, and disclose to customers, such practices.

Sapphires are quite easy to grow in the laboratory or factory and a cheap form of synthetic sapphire was discovered well over 100 years ago. While at first, the cause of color was disputed, the discovery that both titanium and iron had to be present eventually allowed manufacture to begin at a considerable rate. Such specimens, still made on a large scale today, are glassy and so free from solid inclusions that they should arouse immediate suspicion. Other, more expensive, synthetic sapphires are harder to detect but are not very common.

While yellow sapphires often turn up in jewelry, other colors are not quite defined or attractive enough for setting. The exception is the romantically named "padparadschah," found in Sri Lanka. The color of this gem (whatever the books say!) should be a rosy pink, reminiscent of a stage in the color development of the lotus flower. A bright orange, often offered as padparadschah, is not the true variety. Such stones are always indicated in salesroom catalog entries and the name alone is sufficiently well-known among the jewelry-buying public to attract customers.

RINGS

Women and men, in both Eastern and Western cultures, have been wearing rings ever since they were first introduced in the third millennium BC.

This ring, with its rectangular-cut sapphire weighing 31.12 carats, triangular cut diamond shoulders, and 18 carat gold and platinum hoop, is of great interest because the Gübelin Gemmological Laboratory has certified that it comes from Kashmir. Indian sapphires are highly sought after because of their magnificent cornflower blue color, which tends — unlike the hue of other sapphires — to keep its character in the artificial light that these fantastic gems are usually worn in at night. Kashmiri sapphires were first discovered in 1881, when a rockslide in a remote corner of the northwestern Himalayas revealed sapphire-bearing rock. However, in those early days, sapphires were found in such abundance that the local people thought they were semi-precious stones. It was only when they were examined by the gem merchants of Delhi that their true worth was recognized. The Maharajah of Kashmir immediately took an interest in the sapphires and imposed strict licensing on their mining. For many years, the exact location of the mines was a closely guarded secret, kept particularly from Europeans, who were always keen to plunder prodigious mining areas. The area was mined up until the 1930s and

produced some of the most beautiful sapphires the world has ever seen, but the supply has long since dried up. Now, the only source of Kashmiri sapphires is old jewelry, from which the gems must be removed and, sometimes, re-cut to fit modern settings. Sapphires (sapphire is the Greek word for blue) have always been of great significance to past societies. For example, the Mystical Jews regarded the blue gemstones as the secret message from the beyond and the Persians thought the world rested on a giant sapphire, the sky being a reflection of the fabulous color of the stone. Gemmologists, however, think of sapphires simply as aluminum oxide (otherwise known as corundum), which is the same stone, with the exception of color, as the ruby. It is the presence of traces of titanium oxide and iron oxide that give the sapphire its rich blue color.

Estimate: $750,000-850,000; *Magnificent Jewels, Geneva, May 21, 1992*

This dress ring, with a rectangular-cut sapphire weighing 31.37 carats in a pavé-set diamond and beaded stylized crossover mount, was created around 1950 by Jean Schlumberger. Note the "nails" of gold, which were often used as a decorative device on bright enamel and pavé-set stone surfaces. Schlumberger, born in German-controlled Alsace in 1907, was one of the 20th century's most creative jewelry designers. He started off making porcelain flowers mounted on clips and selling them to friends, before moving to Paris in the 1930s and making costume jewelry for the couturier Elsa Schiaparelli. By the late 1930s, he had settled in New York, where, following the end of the Second World War, he opened his own salon selling clothes and jewelry. This time, he used precious and semi-precious materials, but he maintained the exciting elements of fantasy that had characterized his costume jewelry and his pieces were both colorful and exuberant. In 1956, he formed an association with the leading American jeweler's Tiffany and was made head of his own special design department. Eventually, he retired to London, where he died in 1987, but his collection can still be bought from Tiffany to this day.

Estimate:
£30,000-35,000;
Jewellery, London, June 22, 1994

The *Exposition Internationale des Art Decoratifs*, which took place in Paris in 1925, gave the Art Deco movement its name. With its abstract designs and geometric patterns, Art Deco was a direct challenge to the floral, free-flowing work of the earlier Art Nouveau era. This cocktail ring certainly reflects those Art Deco principles. The central cushion-shaped sapphire weighing 3.65 carats is surrounded by a cartouche-shaped panel of calibré-cut sapphires, and old European and baguette-cut diamonds, mounted on a platinum hoop. Cocktail rings are a fairly modern jewelry development, having been popular since the second quarter of the 20th century. They do not have any prescribed form, but are usually large, with an ornate shank (another word for a hoop) and set with a number of stones in a domed shape, so that they cannot easily be worn under a glove.

Estimate: $17,500-22,000; *Important Jewels, St Moritz, February 23/24, 1996*

This simple three-stone ring features a central sapphire weighing 4.16 carats, flanked by two cushion-shaped diamonds, which are set on a plain hoop. A cushion-shaped gem is defined as having either a square or rectangular shape with rounded corners.

Estimate: $20,000-26,000; *Important Jewels, St Moritz, February 23/24, 1996*

The sapphires in this ring have quite an interesting history. They are thought to have been bought from the late Karan Singh, the Maharajah of Kashmir, in London circa 1950-1951, but not before he had offered them to the owner of the famous French racetrack of Deauville. She refused to accept the gift, but the Maharajah was not to be thwarted. He gave them to his friend, Victor Rosenthal, a well-known Parisian pearl dealer, to forward on to her. Once again, she refused, so Rosenthal sold them for £1,500 to the gentleman who put them up for the sale at Christie's in 1996.

The three cut-cornered rectangular-cut sapphires, surrounded by a bombe pavé-set diamond half-hoop surround, were mounted in platinum, which bears French assay marks. Bombe refers to a dome-shaped piece of jewelry.

Estimate: $50,000-60,000; *Magnificent Jewels, Geneva, November 21, 1996*

The heart-shaped sapphire in this cocktail ring is surrounded by a pavé-set diamond mount, set in 18 carat white gold. The sapphire weighs 16.49 carats. Pavé-set refers to the setting, which could be likened to paving stones in that many small gemstones are set very close together so as to cover the entire piece and conceal the metal base. Typically, in order that the gems fit together snugly, calibré-cut diamonds, which are small and oblong or elliptical in shape, are used.

Estimate: $28,000-32,000; *Magnificent Jewels, Geneva, November 21, 1996*

This cushion-shaped pointed cabochon sapphire has a circular-cut diamond bezel (the setting edge of the ring), pear-shaped diamond single-stone shoulders, and a plain hoop. Made by Cartier, the sapphire weighs 18.11 carats. The term cabochon comes from the French word for a doorknob, *caboche*, and refers to the smooth, rounded, and highly polished surface of the sapphire. This type of cut was used centuries ago, before the development of faceting (the cutting of a gemstone), and was only revived during the Art Nouveau era (1890s-early 1900s). Cartier, founded in Paris in 1847 by Louis-François Cartier, was creating jewelry for royalty shortly after its conception and has continued to produce top of the range goods ever since.

Estimate: £150,000-180,000; *Important Jewellery, London, December 13, 1989*

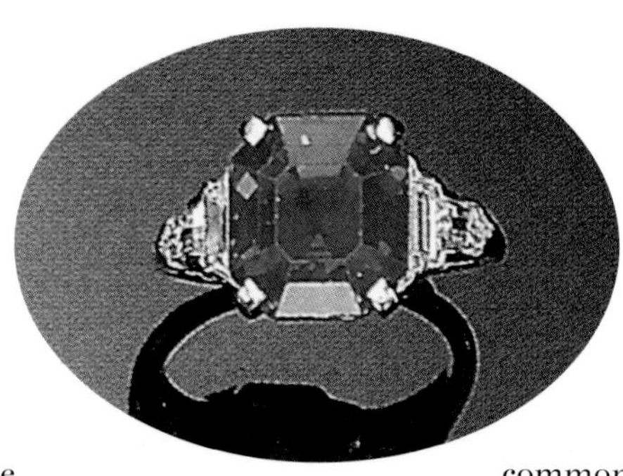

The rectangular-cut Kashmiri sapphire in this ring weighs approximately 7.93 carats and is flanked on either side by a bullet and a trapeze-cut diamond, all of which are mounted in platinum. An accompanying certificate from the American Gemmological Laboratories confirms that the sapphire is from Kashmir and adds that there is no gemmological evidence of heat induced appearance modification. This is important, as it is increasingly common for sapphires to be heat-treated. Once a sapphire is, quite literally, cooked in a furnace, its color is greatly intensified and any inclusions are burnt away. However, it is worth noting that heat treatment is very difficult, sometimes impossible, for an expert to detect. Perhaps as a result, thermally treated stones are generally accepted commercially now, but there will always be a demand for — and a higher price on — completely natural sapphires.

Estimate: $30,000-50,000, *Magnificent Jewels, New York, October 24, 1995*

This cluster ring, set with a cushion-shaped sapphire weighing 12.64 carats in a pear-shaped, marquise and circular cut diamond tiered surround, is mounted in platinum and signed by Chaumet of Paris. It comes with a certificate from the Gübelin Gemmological Laboratory stating that the sapphire is of Burmese origin. Burmese sapphires, which are the next most valuable after those from Kashmir, are much more common than their Indian counterparts. The color of Burmese sapphires tends to be dark and strong, but they also have some of the same velvety quality of Kashmiri gems. One of the top French jewelry houses, Chaumet's early success came about through a stroke of luck.

In the late 18th century, Etienne Nitot, who founded the company, saw an accident outside his shop and, when he rushed out to help, found himself assisting First Consul Napoleon Bonaparte. The latter thanked Nitot by commissioning him to make the Emperor's Coronation Crown and Sword, a tiara given to the Pope, and the jewelry worn by Marie Louise on her marriage to Napoleon in 1810. The firm was appointed jeweler to Louis Philippe 20 years later and its reputation was guaranteed. Chaumet subsequently made jewelry for the courts of Europe, Russia, the Near East, and India.

Estimate: $55,000-70,000, *Magnificent Jewels, Geneva, May 21, 1992*

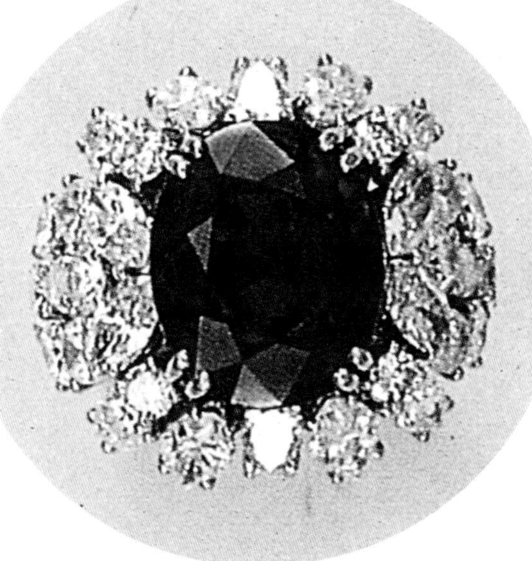

These two rings are a clear indicator that it is not just the carat (or weight) which determines the price of a gemstone — the color, clarity, and cut of the stone are also important. The first has a cushion-shaped sapphire weighing 10.26 carats set off by baguette-cut sapphire line shoulders and a pavé-set diamond tiered surround, and came with an estimate of $20,000-25,000. However, the other, with a larger, rectangular-cut sapphire weighing 12.34 carats in a circular-cut diamond cluster surround, mounted in platinum, came with a lower estimate of between $8,000 and $10,000.

Estimate: *Magnificent Jewels, Geneva, May 21, 1992*

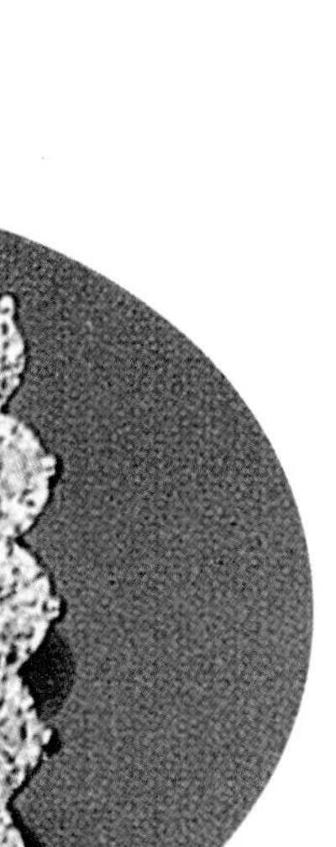

In 1935, Van Cleef & Arpels revolutionized the jewelry world by introducing the "invisible setting." In other words, it managed to find a way to mount gemstones without any visible sign of a setting. This invisibly set sapphire bombe band with an 18 carat gold hoop is a good example of its work. Van Cleef & Arpels, a leading French jewelry house that was founded in 1906, is also famous for creating the *minaudière*, a sleek gold box with hidden compartments that was said to hold all the essential items for a well-dressed lady. In response to a more casual lifestyle, the company also developed a less expensive "Boutique" range, a concept that has subsequently been copied by other top class jewelers.

Estimate: $10,000-12,5000, *Magnificent Jewels, Geneva, May 18, 1995*

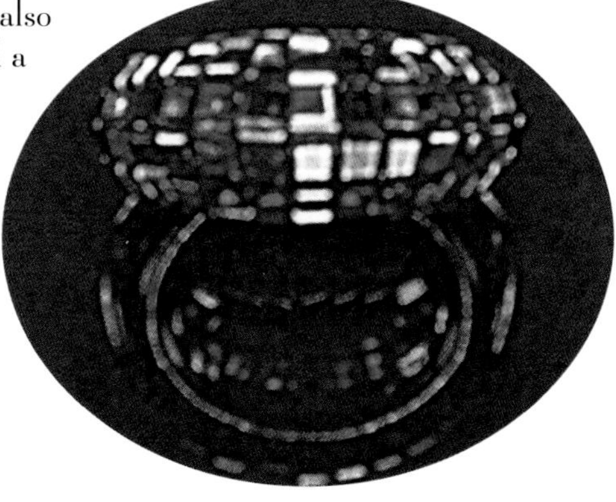

Here is further evidence of the great difference in price that a quality stone can make to a piece of jewelry. While the 48.24 carat cabochon sapphire and diamond ring on the right was put up for auction with an estimate of $12,000-15,000, the ring on the left, with a 30.68 cushion-shaped sapphire, was expected to sell for between $240,000 and $280,000. The latter had the advantage of being created by the

well-known Italian firm of Bulgari and was accompanied by a certificate from the SSEF Swiss Gemmological Institute stating that the sapphire is of Burmese origin and shows no sign of thermal treatment.

Estimate: (1) $12,000-15,000; Important Jewels, New York, December 9, 1996 (2) $240,000-280,000; *Magnificent Jewels, Geneva, November 21, 1996*

BRACELETS

BRACELETS

Men and women have been wearing bracelets since very early times. Although they lost popularity in the Middle Ages and the Renaissance, due to the long sleeves that were then fashionable, bracelets have enjoyed something of a revival since the 18th and 19th centuries.

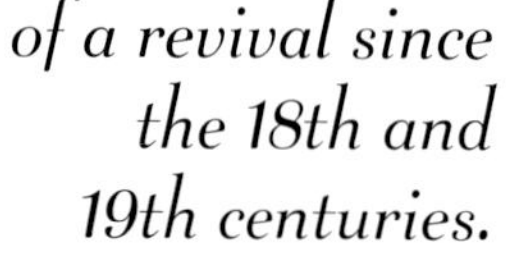

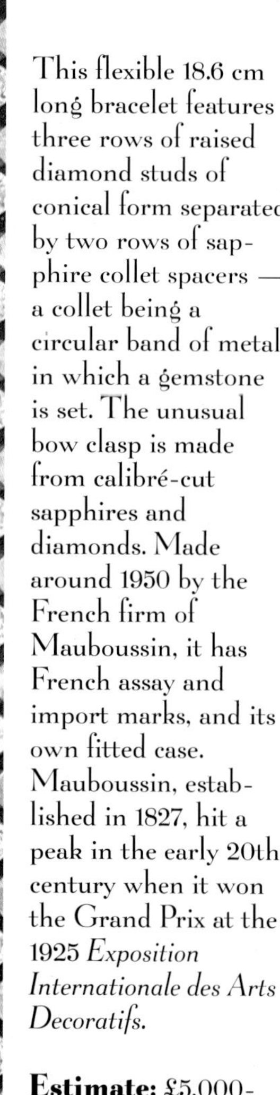

This flexible 18.6 cm long bracelet features three rows of raised diamond studs of conical form separated by two rows of sapphire collet spacers — a collet being a circular band of metal in which a gemstone is set. The unusual bow clasp is made from calibré-cut sapphires and diamonds. Made around 1950 by the French firm of Mauboussin, it has French assay and import marks, and its own fitted case. Mauboussin, established in 1827, hit a peak in the early 20th century when it won the Grand Prix at the 1925 *Exposition Internationale des Arts Decoratifs.*

Estimate: £5,000-7,000; *Jewellery, London, June 22, 1994*

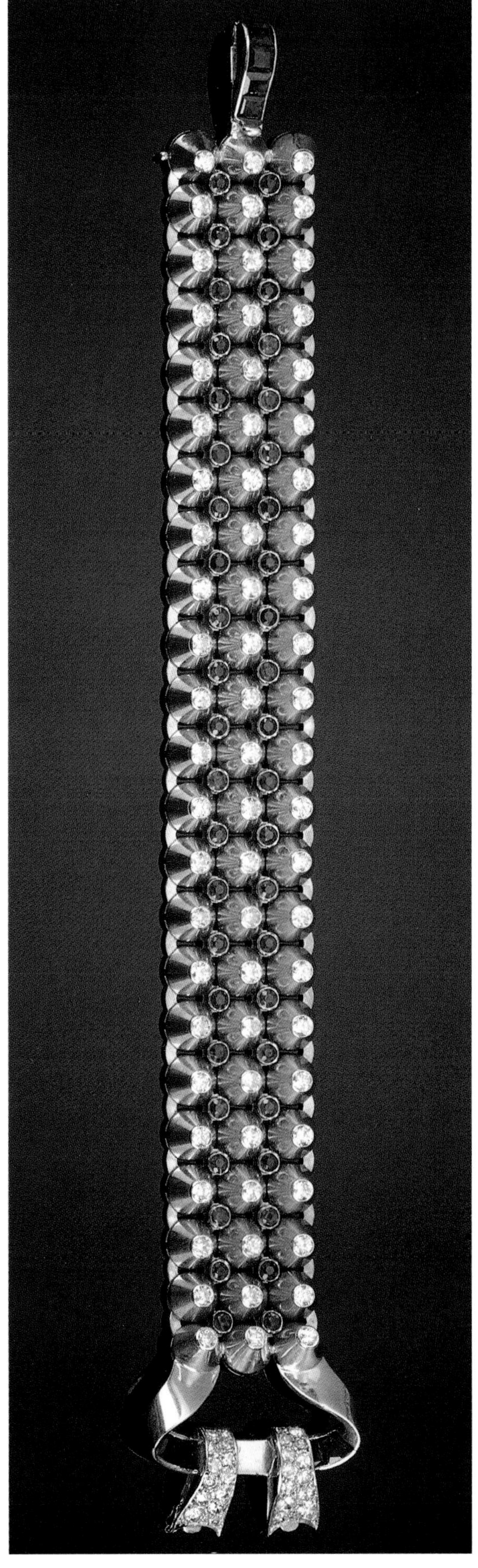

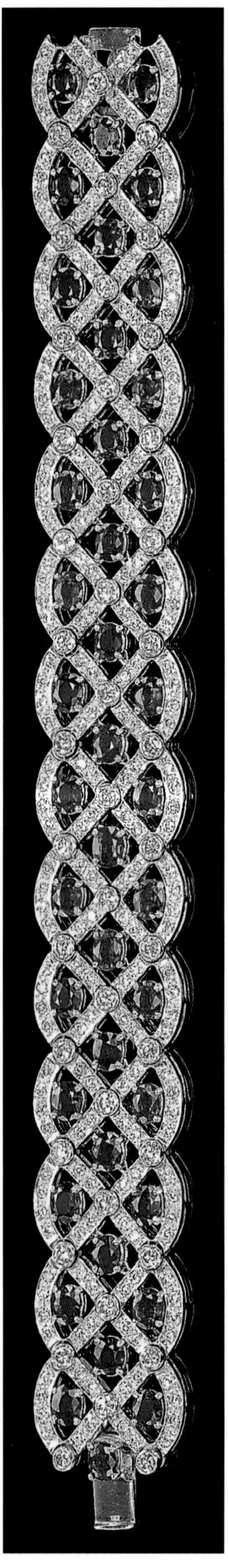

This bracelet is similar in concept to the one above in that it is a flexible 18 cm long bracelet with diamond collet and cushion-shaped sapphire spacers, but the pavé-set diamond band of lattice motif gives it a completely different look.

Estimate: $10,500-14,000; *Important Jewels, St Moritz, February 23/24, 1996*

Attached to this 18 carat white gold charm bracelet are six charms of various motifs set with diamonds, sapphires, rubies, tsavorite garnets, and black onyx. Charm bracelets are first believed to have come into existence in the 19th century, but they were not widely worn until the early 20th century. Traditionally, the charms were worn to bring good luck to the wearer and ward off evil spirits, but nowadays, they are more likely to reflect the owner's interests or recent holiday destinations.

Estimate: $4,000-4,800; *Important Jewels, St Moritz, February 23/24, 1996*

From time to time, Christie's finds itself selling a gem or piece of jewelry for the second, or even third, time. For example, this Aletto bracelet was in the Magnificent Jewels sale held in Geneva on May 21, 1992, with an estimate of $40,000-50,000, before re-appearing in the New York sale three years later. Composed of four rows of invisibly set calibré-cut sapphires, it is bordered by diamond collets.
A calibré-cut gem is one that has been cut into a shape, usually oblong or elliptical, so that it will fit snugly into clusters with other gems cut in the same manner.
The result in this instance is a bracelet resembling a very symmetrical cobblestone street and a highly flexible band that is held in place by a baguette-cut diamond clasp.
Albert Aletto, a third generation jeweler, was apprenticed to his family's business in Italy at the age of 13. Once he had learnt all he needed to know, he emigrated to South America and established several jewelry factories that are still in existence today. In 1964, he moved to New York, where he opened his own shop. Since the mid-1980s, his four sons have been in charge of the business, which has now relocated to Florida. There, they specialize in top notch, invisibly set jewelry — such as this one — that is entirely handmade.

Estimate: $40,000-50,000; *Magnificent Jewels, New York, October 24, 1995*

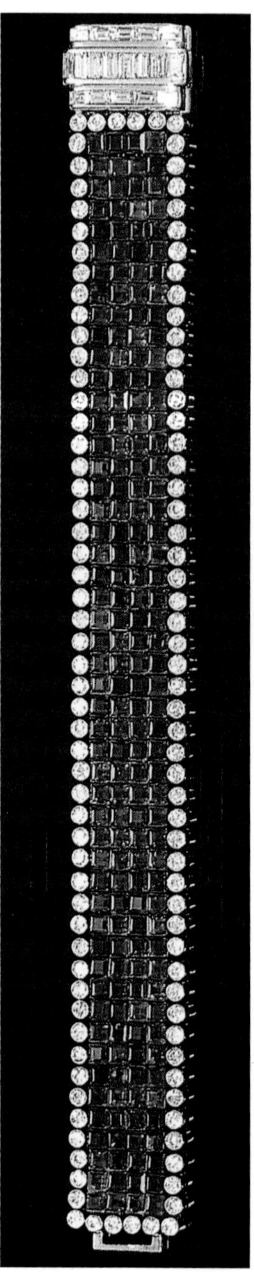

And then there are times when Christie's sells a piece that looks just like another piece, but in fact is not. Such is the case with this bracelet. Virtually identical to the Aletto piece, this bracelet by Van Cleef & Arpels appears to differ only in its length: according to the measurements provided in the Christie's catalogs, it is half a centimeter longer than the Aletto one. And, of course, the price differs too. Perhaps it was just a case of inflation, but it may have also been the Van Cleef & Arpels name that pushed the estimate up by some 25 percent.

Estimate: $50,000-67,000; *Magnificent Jewels, Geneva, November 20, 1997*

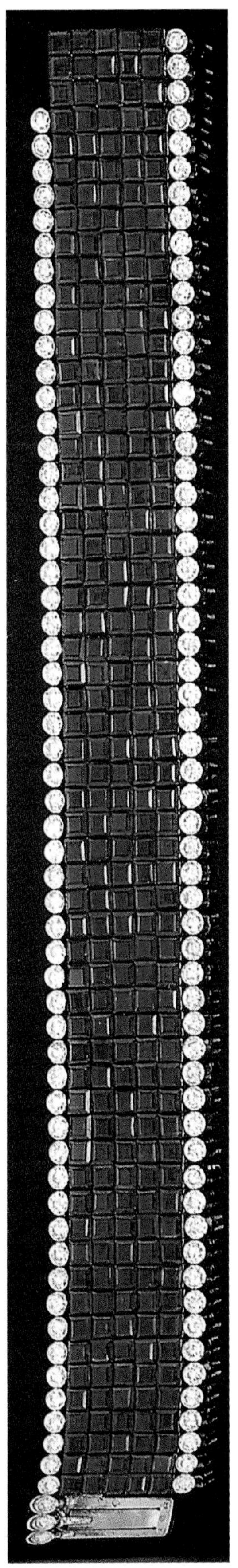

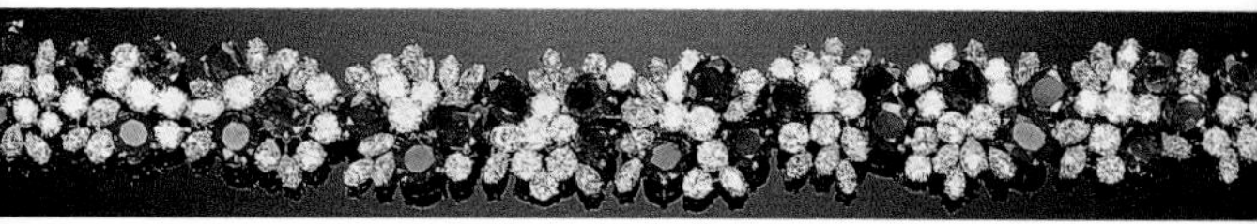

The bracelet above, which resembles a flower chain, is made from a series of oval-cut sapphire and circular and marquise-cut diamond clusters. Mounted in platinum, it measures 18.4 cm in length, while the total estimated weights of the sapphires and diamonds are approximately 30 and 22 carats, respectively.

Estimate: $35,000-45,000; *Magnificent Jewels, New York, October 24, 1995*

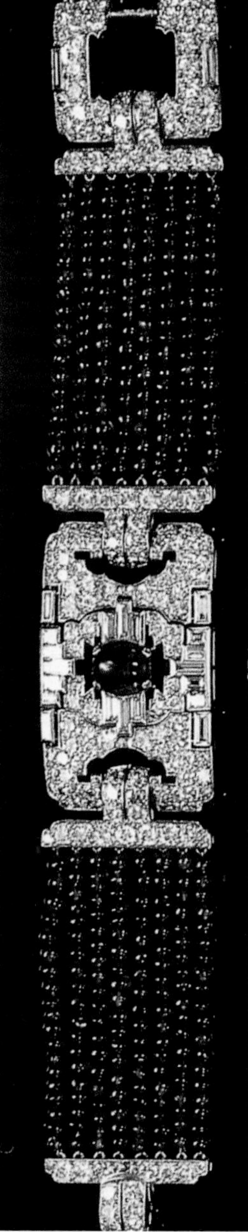

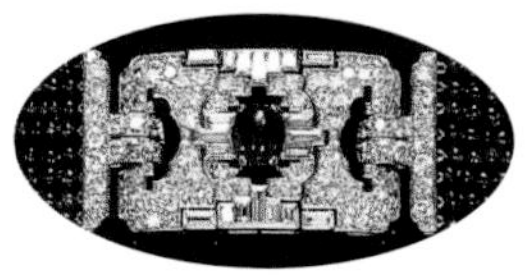

The centerpiece of this Art Deco sapphire and diamond bracelet is a pavé-set diamond articulated openwork panel, which is enhanced by a central cabochon sapphire, and baguette-cut diamonds. Eight strands of small sapphire beads connect the panel to a baguette and old European-cut diamond buckle clasp. The 16.5 cm long bracelet is mounted in platinum, which bears French hallmarks that attest to both the purity of the metal and the date when the bracelet was made — about 1925.

Estimate: $18,000-22,000; *Magnificent Jewels, New York, April 9, 1997*

This elegant, slim Art Deco bracelet has four rectangular-cut sapphire, baguette-cut and pavé-set diamond buckle links, with diamond collet intersections. Mounted in platinum, it is 18 cm long, was made circa 1925, and has French assay marks, which, like a hallmark, affirm the purity of the metal used.

Estimate: $15,000-18,500; *Magnificent Jewels, Geneva, May 18, 1995*

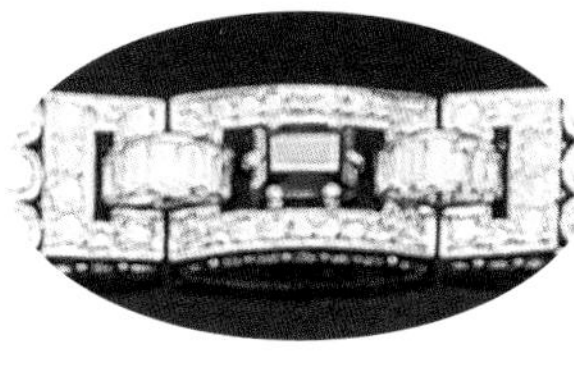

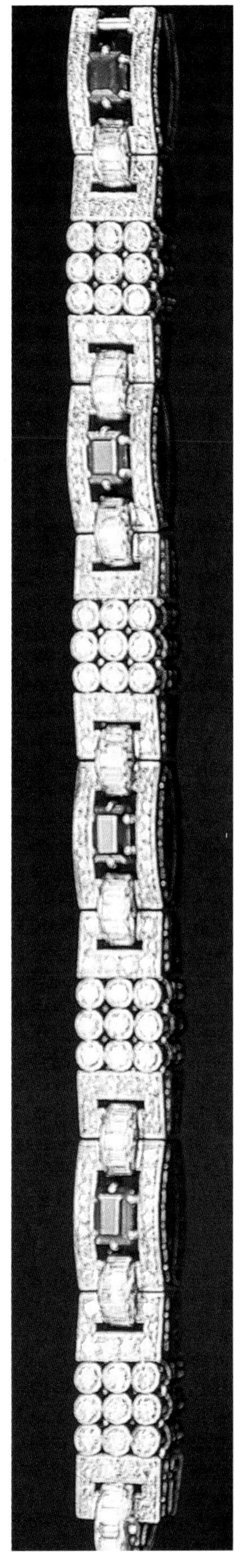

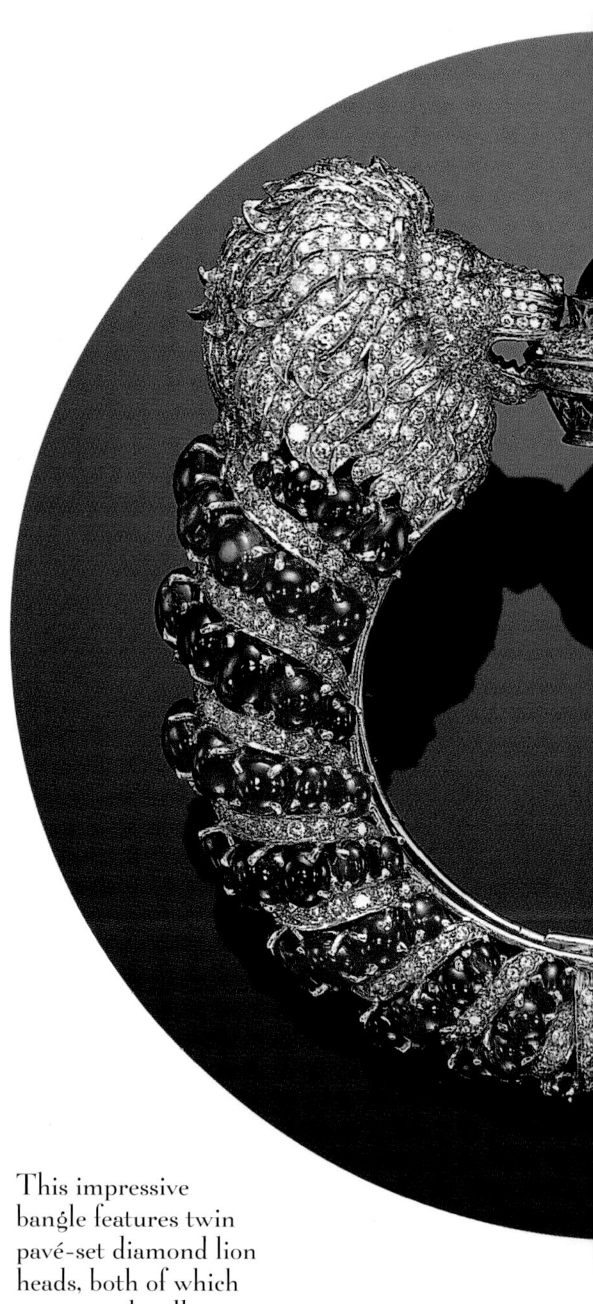

This impressive bangle features twin pavé-set diamond lion heads, both of which are set with yellow diamond eyes. Between them, they hold a cabochon sapphire surrounded by diamonds in their mouths. Their bodies, encrusted with cabochon rubies and sapphires, plus diamonds, form the hinged hoop of the bangle — a bangle differs from a bracelet in that it is rigid.

Estimate: $25,000-30,000; *Important Jewels, New York, December 9, 1996*

NECKLACES

NECKLACES

Necklaces, worn since time immemorial, come in all shapes and sizes. Closely fitting necklaces are usually referred to as chokers, while long, free-flowing ones are known as neck chains or sautoirs. While some are heavily laden with gems, others may be a more simple pendant.

Having said that, there would have been nothing simple about the original chain on which this huge pendant once hung. In the midst of a circular-cut diamond surround and an old mine-cut diamond 16 stone border with four larger diamond collets at the cardinal points, lies a cushion-shaped sapphire weighing 337.66 carats. Sapphires of this size, color, and clarity are incredibly rare. The two largest sapphires in the world are the amusingly named "Peter the Great's Nose," a huge cabochon of 548 carats which is now in the Green Vault in Dresden, and the "Star of India," which weighs 536 carats and is found in the American Museum of Natural History. The world's largest cut sapphire, weighing 478 carats, was mounted as the pendant in a sautoir. Cartier exhibited it in 1919, when numerous monarchs and heads of state expressed an interest in it. But it was King Ferdinand of Romania who eventually bought it for his consort, Queen Maria. She had previously refused to buy any jewelry as nothing

matched the pieces in her collection, much of which had belonged to her mother, the Duchess of Saxe Coburg-Gotha. However, the sautoir was the perfect match for a sapphire tiara the Queen had bought from Grand Duchess Vladimir after she left Russia. There is then only one other sapphire greater than this one in existence and that is the "Logan Sapphire" in Washington's Smithsonian Institute, which weighs 423 carats.

However, another sapphire does exist which is the same size as this one; it is called "Catherine the Great." The family that sold the sapphire was a long standing client of the French firm of Cartier, which mounted the stone in circa 1910, around the time when great transactions and masterful creations were the preserve of the firm.

Estimate: $850,000-1,100,000; *Magnificent Jewels, Geneva, May 16, 1991*

In comparison to the piece on the previous page, the heart-shaped sapphire in this pendant appears relatively small, but it is still an impressive 132.27 carats. According to an accompanying certificate from the Gübelin Gemmological Laboratory, the sapphire is of Burmese origin.

Estimate: $250,000-300,000; *Magnificent Jewels, Geneva, May 21, 1992*

This is an unusual, but very elegant, Art Deco double pendant, which is designed as two single-cut diamond drop-shaped pendants. Each one features a marquise-cut sapphire and cushion-shaped emerald floret, and has diamond collet accents. The two pendants are suspended by articulated lines of old mine-cut diamonds and circular-cut sapphires and emeralds from a diamond, sapphire, and emerald bail of similar design. Mounted in both platinum and gold, the pendant comes with French

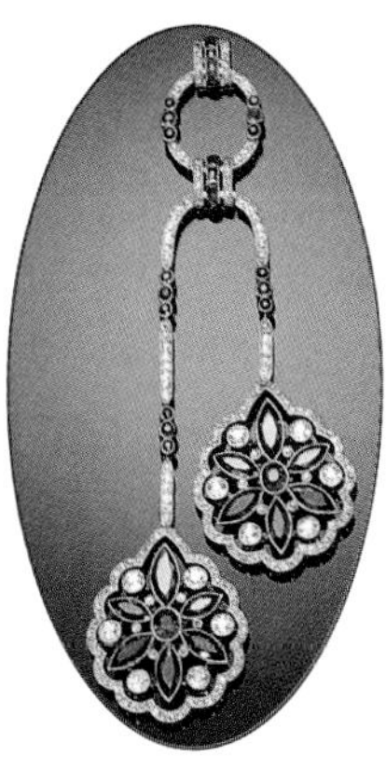

hallmarks dating to around 1925 and a maker's mark for Picq. This latter mark is interesting, because Picq was the name of a workshop to which Cartier used to farm out work. Why? Well, in the first quarter of the 20th century, Paris was the center of the jewelry world and clients were clamoring for pieces from the legendary firms of Cartier, Van Cleef & Arpels, and Boucheron. In the case of Cartier, demand was so intense that occasionally they asked outside workshops either to finish an object that required a specialized technique, such as enameling, or to manufacture the entire piece. Picq was one of Cartier's favorites. Unfortunately, Picq no longer exists, for the caliber of its work, as illustrated by this exquisite pendant, is a quintessential reflection of the truly amazing workmanship that was crafted during this thrilling era.

Estimate: $40,000-50,000; *Magnificent Jewels, New York, April 9, 1997*

This pendant cross has an interesting provenance, having been the property of a European royal family. It originally belonged to Queen Alexandrine of Denmark, who died in 1952, and was passed down through the family, via HRH Princess Caroline-Mathilde, to the owner who sold it through Christie's in 1996.

Cruciform pendants were usually made in a Latin cross or, like this one, a cross with four arms of equal length; decoration was provided either by engravings or gemstones. This particular cross is set with a central cushion-cut diamond, while the four arms are set with cushion-shaped sapphires, rubies, and yellow and brown diamonds, with rose-cut diamond border details. Pearl

pendant drops hang from three of the arms and the fourth is topped with a trefoil colored diamond pendant loop. Mounted in gold in around 1890, the cross measures 9 cm in height.

Estimate: £10,000-12,000/$16,000-19,000; *Christie's Antique Jewellery, Antique Jewels and Rings, London, October 9, 1996*

This sapphire and diamond pendant necklace is of interest because it used to belong to the socialite Vera Hue-Williams. Born Vera Sklarevskia in Kiev at the turn of the century, she fled the Russian Revolution, along with her sister Olga and her mother Baroness Kostovesky, in 1917, arriving in Paris with very few possessions other than the jewels hidden in her clothes.

At 17, the stunningly beautiful Vera married an Englishman, who died ten years later. Her second husband, Walter Sherwin Cottingham, whom she married in 1931, owned the Lewis Berger Paint Company. When he died five years later, she inherited his fortune. During the Second World War, Vera married Thomas Lilley, chairman of the shoe company Lilley & Skinner. Together, they set up the Woolton House Stud at their home in Woolton Hill near Newbury. Even in the glamorous world of horse racing, Vera was a leading light. Not only that, she was also a winner. Her horses triumphed in several important races, including the first running of the King George VI and Queen Elizabeth Stakes in 1951. Four years after Lilley died in 1959, Vera wed — for the fourth and final time — Colonel Roger Hue-Williams, who was to die in 1987.

Throughout her life, Vera traveled extensively, visiting friends, attending to her business interests, and enjoying holidays in some of the world's most exclusive resorts. All of these activities demanded glamorous clothes and expensive jewels. Vera's jewelry, much of it designed

and made in the 1930s, was always of the finest quality even if the design was very simple.
The pendant, a 68.42 carat cushion-shaped sapphire surrounded by a two-tiered old European-cut diamond cluster attached to the main part of the necklace by a marquise-cut diamond, is detachable.

The graduated cushion-shaped sapphire and old European-cut diamond cluster necklace, which measures 35.5 cm in length, has roughly 80 carats of sapphires and 45 carats of diamonds.

Estimate: $500,000-670,000; *The Magnificent Jewels of Vera Hue-Williams, Geneva, May 18, 1995*

Pendant necklaces have been popular since 1850, so although this one does not bear a date, it is unlikely to be more than 150 years old. The nine-strand sapphire bead necklace with cabochon emerald and

circular-cut diamond flowerhead spacers is certainly unusual. With a central section consisting of a pavé-set diamond, cabochon emerald and sapphire quatrefoil cluster, from which hang a series of detachable sapphire bead tassels with diamond and cabochon sapphire bail, this necklace almost looks ethnic. Mounted in 18 carat gold, it is 41 cm long.

Estimate: $23,000-26,000; *Magnificent Jewels, Geneva, November 21, 1996*

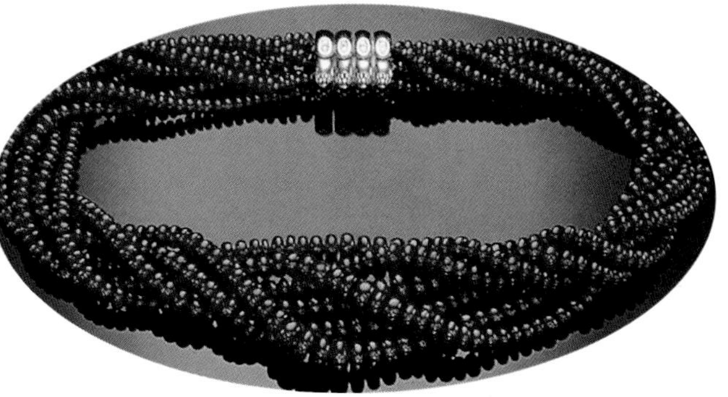

This sapphire torsade necklace, with its six graduated sapphire bead strands and ribbed gold clasp with pavé-set diamond detail, is a much simpler version of the previous necklace.

Estimate: $12,000-15,000; *Magnificent Jewels, Geneva, November 15, 1995*

This quite remarkable looking piece belongs to the Art Nouveau era, which dominated the 1890s and early 1900s, before it fizzled out at the start of the Great War and was replaced by Art Deco. The movement was named after an interior decoration shop called the "Maison de l'Art Nouveau," which opened in Paris in 1896. However, the term was applied to all the decorative arts, including jewelry. Its main features were free-flowing, curving lines, with asymmetrical motifs representing nature, such as intertwining floral patterns (think William Morris), butterflies, dragonflies, and ethereal female faces.

A very adaptable piece of jewelry, it can be worn either as a pendant necklace or as a 12.5 cm high brooch pendant and two 18 cm long bracelets. Hanging from the crescent-shaped central section of the flattened running foliate necklace, which is set with cabochon sapphires, is an elongated foliate drop with a star sapphire center. Made around 1900, the necklace bears French assay marks.

Estimate: £11,000-13,000, *Important Jewellery, London, June 21, 1995*

The cluster pendant in this necklace by Van Cleef & Arpels is set with marquise-cut sapphires and circular and marquise-cut diamonds, which are joined to a necklace set with a line of oval-cut sapphires, each surrounded by pear and circular-cut diamonds. The total weight of the ten oval-cut sapphires is approximately 13.90 carats.

Estimate: $40,000-60,000; *Magnificent Jewels, New York, October 24, 1995*

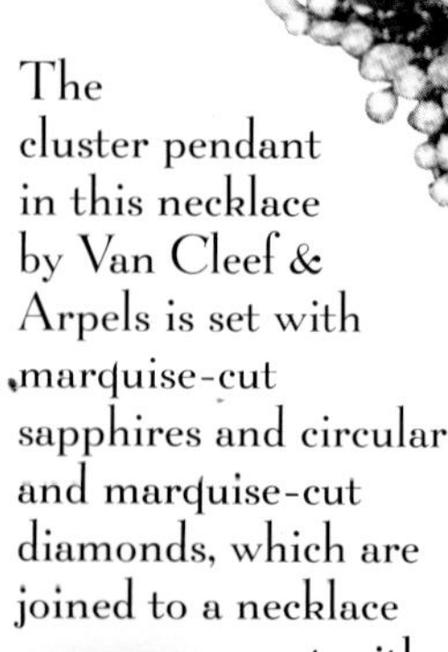

The focal point of this necklace is the oval star sapphire measuring approximately 23 x 19.5 x 14.5 mm. A star sapphire is one that has a silky structure and when cut as a cabochon shows a six, or on the rare occasion 12, pronged star in reflected light; this is the result of an optical phenomenon known as asterism. To ensure a perfect star shape, the stone has to be precisely cut and aligned with the vertical axis, otherwise the star will be off-center, crooked, dim, or will not appear at all. The star sapphire is set in a circular-cut diamond and hammered gold scroll frame, which hangs on a hammered gold scroll link chain. Note that the four front links on either side have been enhanced by cushion and circular-cut sapphires and diamonds.

Estimate: $12,000-15,000; *Important Jewels, New York, December 9, 1996*

This 18 carat gold, gem-set elephant sautoir, made in about 1940, is instantly recognizable as the work of René Boivin because it is so innovative. And while his jewels were always ahead of their time, they were simultaneously timeless. Sculpted pieces, like this elephant, were also a trademark. The gold elephant is set with diamond eyes and toes, a baroque pearl head, and ruby and diamond details. On its back is a sapphire, diamond, and ruby howdah. It is suspended from a gold rope chain.

Estimate: $16,000-19,000; *Magnificent Jewels, Geneva, November 21, 1996*

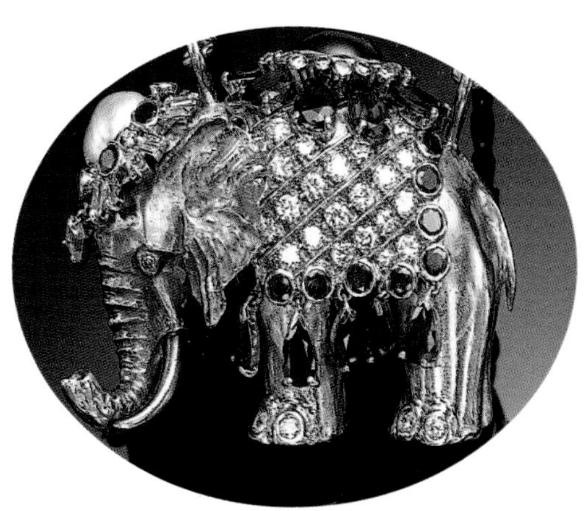

The delicate necklace above and below is the work of one of France's leading jewelry houses, Cartier. Made circa 1930, it features three oval-shaped sapphire and diamond open-work clusters with baguette-cut diamond detail strung into a chain of collet and scroll intersections.

Estimate: £10,000-12,000; *Jewellery, London, June 22, 1994*

The sapphire and diamond necklace on the right was created by the Paris-based jewelry house Boucheron in 1950. Boucheron was founded at the Palais Royale in 1858 by Frédéric Boucheron, who soon acquired a reputation as a precious stones expert, a masterful technician, and a creator of beautiful jewelry designs. The company remains in family hands to this day.

The front section of the necklace has seven graduated cushion-shaped sapphires, each set in a baguette and circular-cut diamond ribbon surround, which are attached to a diamond necklace.

Estimate: $30,000-39,000; *Important Jewels, St Moritz, February 23/24, 1996*

Around 1935, Bulgari made this festoon necklace with its five rows of graduated cushion-shaped sapphire, circular and old European-cut diamonds; collet-set baguette, circular, and bullet-cut diamond lattice shoulders; pear-shaped sapphire, pear-shaped and circular-cut diamond ribbon terminals; and diamond bar clasp. It comes with a certificate from the Gübelin Gemmological Laboratory confirming that 15 of the sapphires were picked at random and, in their opinion, nine were determined to be of Burmese origin. The firm of Bulgari was founded by Sotirio Bulgari, who was born in 1857 in Greece, but later emigrated to Naples, and finally made his name in Rome. Upon Sotirio's death in 1932, his sons Giorgio and Constantine took over the business. The former is credited with creating the highly distinctive Bulgari style, which, inspired by classical and Renaissance art, features colors and patterns found in mosaics and, at times, ancient coins. Bulgari remains a family concern, with Paolo and Nicola, the two sons of Giorgio, running the company.

Estimate: $320,000-400,000; *Magnificent Jewels, Geneva, November 21, 1996*

Glancing at this multi-colored bib necklace by Della Valle, not many would know that all the gems are sapphires, for it is a common misconception that sapphires are always blue. They actually come in a wide range of colors, from deep blue to yellow, green, brown, pink, purple, and the very rare orange-pink sapphire known as "Padparadschah." Non-blue sapphires are referred to as "fancy-colored." While the rich blue color of a sapphire is the result of traces of titanium oxide and iron oxide, the color in violet sapphires derives from vanadium, in yellow and green stones from iron, and in pink stones from chromium. Some sapphires may even be "white" or "colorless." This particular necklace features pink, blue, and yellow oval-shaped sapphires, mounted in 18 carat gold.

Estimate: $13,000-15,000, *Magnificent Jewels, Geneva, November 15, 1995*

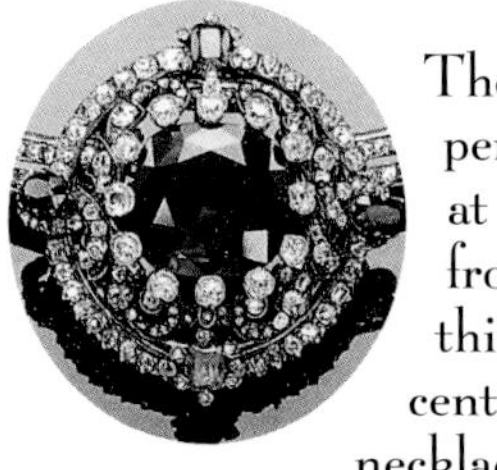

The pendant at the front of this 19th century necklace, which formerly belonged to the Duc de la Rochefoucault, can be removed. An old mine-cut diamond cluster surrounds the sapphire, which weighs 15.31 carats. The pendant itself is flanked by four pear-shaped sapphire pendants, all of which hang from a rose-cut diamond twin-row necklace with cushion-shaped sapphire and diamond cluster spacers.

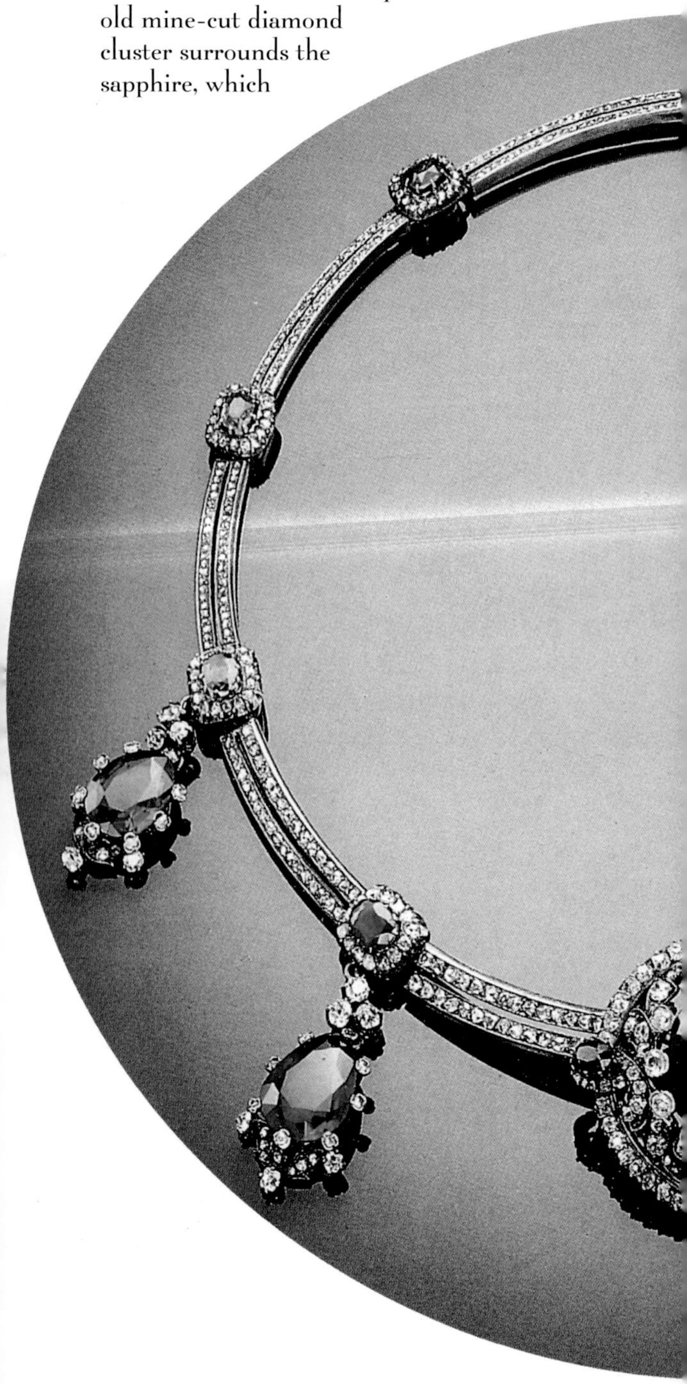

Poetically named rose-cut diamonds are cut in a symmetrical form, with the facets being of various shapes and relative sizes, but characteristically having a flat base and two horizontal rows of facets rising to a point. It is an old style of cut, having been developed by Dutch lapidaries in the mid-17th century.

Estimate: $100,000-125,000; *Magnificent Jewels, Geneva, May 18, 1995*

SUITES

Suite is the modern name for a parure, a set of — for example — necklace, bracelet, brooch, and earrings, which are made of the same kind of gems and are designed to be worn all at the same time. Parures became fashionable towards the end of the 16th century and were revived in the 19th century. Traditionally, they are made with diamonds for formal wear and other precious stones for day wear.

This suite of sapphire and diamond jewelry belonged to one Mildred S. Hilson, but is probably better known for having been worn by President's wife Barbara Bush. Hilson, who died in 1994 at the age of 96, was the widow of Edwin I. Hilson, an investment banker who died in 1952. She was one of the last of a generation of grand dames who made New York society so vibrant in the late 20th century. Her charitable efforts raised millions of dollars for the Hospital for Special Surgery and the American Cancer Society. A true Republican, she befriended every Republican president from Dwight D. Eisenhower to George Bush — at her 90th birthday party, Richard Nixon played the piano and sang "Happy Birthday" to her. Her home and clothes showed impeccable taste, which extended to her jewels — they were always of the highest quality and design. This David Webb suite consists of four pieces: a necklace, ear clips, bracelet, and ring sold in three lots.

The three clusters on the necklace detach to form brooches. These clusters, made with carved cabochon and faceted sapphires, are interspersed with circular-cut diamonds. Each is enhanced by pavé-set diamond foliate motifs, joined to a similarly set tapering back chain, mounted in platinum and 14 carat white gold.

Estimate: $40,000-50,000 (necklace and ear rings); *Magnificent Jewels, New York, October 24, 1995*

David Webb arrived in New York in 1941, at the age of 16, to learn all about jewelry design. Five years later, he and his business partner, Nina Silberstein, opened David Webb Inc. By the early 1950s, they were doing well and had built up a stable of private clients. Although Webb died in 1975, the firm, still under the direction of the Silberstein family, continues to produce jewelry from Webb's vast collection of sketches.

The focus of the sapphire and diamond bracelet is a large bombe cluster of carved, cabochon and faceted sapphires, interspersed with circular-cut diamonds, which, like the necklace, are enhanced by pavé-set diamond foliate motifs. The graduated sapphire bead four-strand band, however, differs slightly from the necklace in that it is mounted in platinum and 18 carat white gold.

Estimate: $15,000-20,000; *Magnificent Jewels, New York, October 24, 1995*

The oval cabochon sapphire in the ring measures approximately 20.7 x 13.2 x 11.10 mm. It is set within an oval cushion and marquise-cut sapphire, circular diamond, and platinum bombe mount, and has an expandable hoop.

Estimate:
$10,000-15,000;
Magnificent Jewels, New York, October 24, 1995

The magnificent sapphires in this suite are associated with the collection of the late Shah of Iran. Jewels and ceremony have always been an integral part of the magnificent Persian culture, and the Royal collection has always been considered one of the world's finest. For example, the Pahlavi Crown, made in 1925 for the coronation of Reza Shah Pahlavi, is set with 3,380 diamonds, 369 matching pearls, and five emeralds that total 199 carats in weight. And when Farah Diba married Mohammed Reza Pahlavi, the future Shah of Iran, in 1959, her wedding tiara included the "Nur-ul-Ain," the world's largest rose pink diamond and widely acknowledged as one of the world's most spectacular gem stones. The necklace in this suite has a central, cushion-cut sapphire weighing approximately 25.54 carats, and is flanked on each wide by two graduated cushion-cut sapphires weighing approximately 5.20, 4.49, 3.21, and 2.23 carats. All are set within marquise-cut diamond floral frames, which are linked to a marquise-cut diamond graduating back chain that is closed by a marquise-cut diamond clasp set with a cushion-cut sapphire weighing approximately 1.96 carats. Certificates from the American Gemmological Laboratories confirm that the sapphires are from Kashmir, the small Indian state that is recognized as the source of the world's finest gems.

Estimate: $800,000-1,000,000; *Magnificent Jewels, New York, October 24, 1995*

The matching sapphire and diamond ear clips are set with cushion-cut sapphires, one weighing 12.26 carats, and the other 10.69 carats. Both are set within a marquise and circular-cut diamond frame, and are mounted in platinum and 18 carat gold. Once again, an American Gemmological Laboratories certificate states that the sapphires are of Kashmiri origin.

Estimate: $300,000-500,000; *Magnificent Jewels, New York, October 24, 1995*

The design for this necklace and bracelet suite looks as though it came from a snake wrapping itself around the branch of a tree. However, Christie's description of the jewelry is much more straightforward: "a circular-cut diamond twin-line band with cushion-shaped sapphire meandering ribbon detail." While the necklace is 38 cms long, the bracelet is 19.5 cms in length; both are set in platinum. Europeans first discovered platinum in the mid-18th century in South America, but they did not start using it to make jewelry until the 19th century. A silver-gray color, it is very strong and malleable, but is the rarest and most expensive of precious metals, hence why it is only used for producing very fine jewelry.

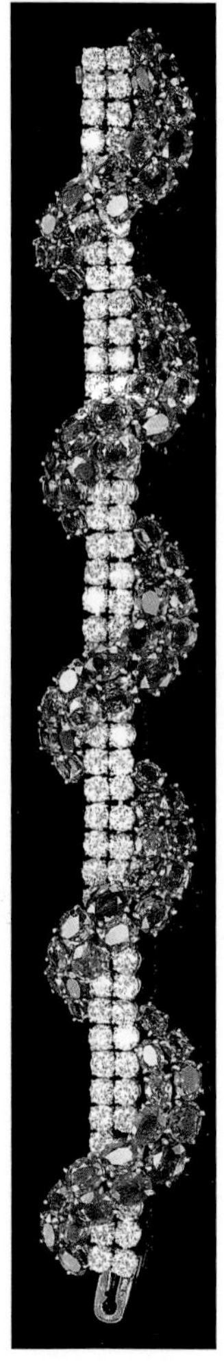

Estimate: $96,000-110,000; *Magnificent Jewels, Geneva, November 21, 1996*

A choker is usually described as a short, narrow necklace worn tight against a woman's throat; if it is short and wide, it becomes known as a dog collar. The necklace in this suite of Van Cleef & Arpels sapphire and diamond jewelry, which was sold by the estate of Marc Haas, is referred to as a choker set with three rows of calibré-cut sapphires and bordered by square-cut diamonds. Like the matching pair of half-loop ear clips, the choker is mounted in 18 carat gold.

Estimate: $40,000-50,000; *Magnificent Jewels, New York, October 24, 1995*

This suite of sapphire and diamond jewelry, created by M. Gérard, consists of a tiara and a pair of ear clips. The front section of the tiara features a circular-cut diamond and cushion-shaped sapphire scrolled oriental motif, which is attached to a circular-cut diamond single row base. Mounted in 18 carat gold, the total weight of the diamonds is said to be 42.97 carats, while the total weight of the sapphires is 29.83 carats.

M. Gérard was founded in 1968 by Louis Gerard, who had worked for a long time, and risen to the position of General Manager, at Van Cleef & Arpels. Eight years later, the company was, and remains, France's largest exporter of top class jewelry.

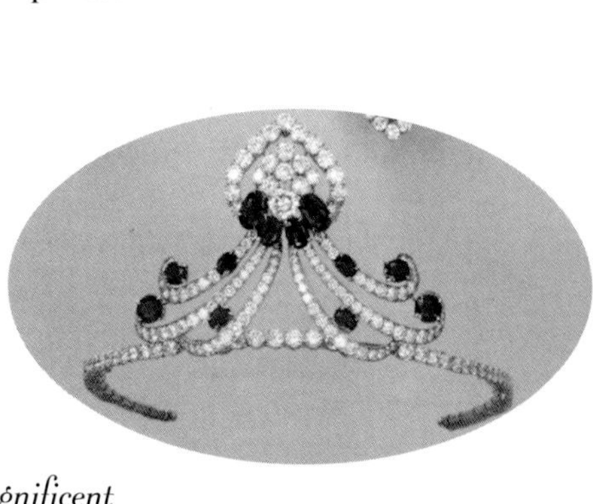

Estimate: $50,000-60,000;*Magnificent Jewels, Geneva, May 21, 1992*

Technically, a suite that only features a couple of pieces of jewelry is known as a demi-parure. This one comprises a necklace with a series of graduated cushion-shaped sapphires, each one separated by a circular-cut diamond five-stone intersection, and a pair of ear clips.

Estimate: $140,000-170,000; *Magnificent Jewels, Geneva, May 27, 1993*

Although not sold by Christie's as a suite, these pieces could quite easily be worn together, so alike are they in their design. The tassel ear pendants each have a cushion-shaped sapphire and circular-cut diamond quatre-foil cluster mount, from which hang three sapphire and diamond cluster tassels with diamond collet intersections.

Estimate: $20,000-23,000; *Magnificent Jewels, Geneva, May 27, 1993*

The necklace is made from alternating cushion-shaped sapphires set in a circular-cut diamond cluster surround, and plain cushion-shaped sapphires. From the main necklace hangs a sapphire and diamond festoon of the same style.

Estimate: $45,000-55,000; *Magnificent Jewels, Geneva, May 27, 1993*

The ring is set with a cushion-shaped sapphire of 3.42 carats and circular-cut diamond cluster surround.

Estimate: $7,000-10,000; *Magnificent Jewels, Geneva, May 27, 1993*

Finally, the bracelet

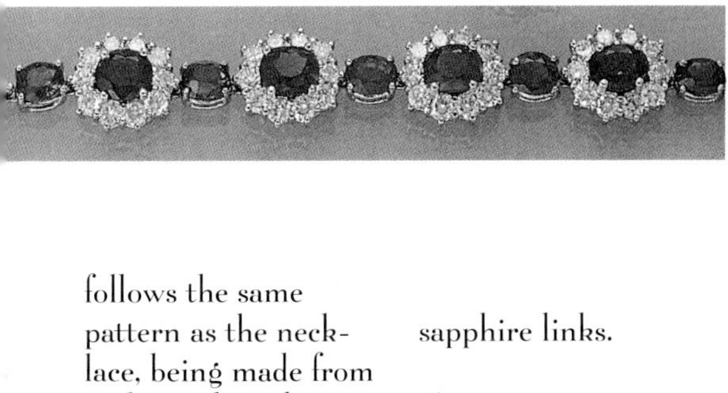

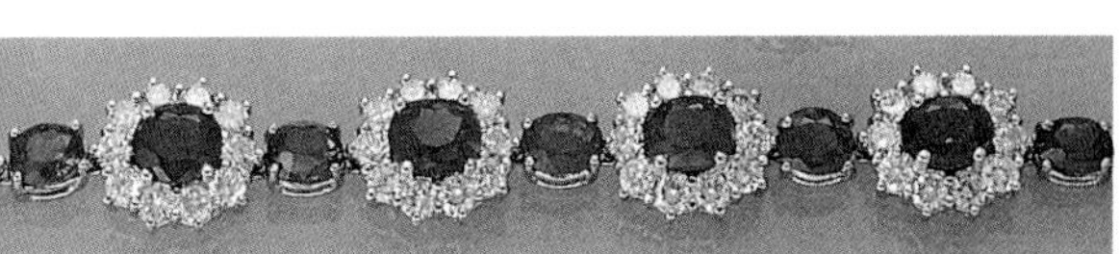

follows the same pattern as the necklace, being made from cushion-shaped sapphire and circular-cut diamond clusters interspersed with cushion-shaped sapphire links.

Estimate: $10,000-13,000; *Magnificent Jewels, Geneva, May 27, 1993*

This suite is very typical of the distinctive Bulgari style, inspired by classical and Renaissance art, that was developed by Giorgio Bulgari earlier this century. The necklace has a front section with three graduated cushion-shaped pink and purple sapphire festoons, featuring ruby spacers and pear-shaped diamond shoulders. The torsade twin-strand necklace is made from colored seed pearls and gold boules. The bracelet and ear pendants are similar in design to the front section of the necklace.

Estimate:
$100,000-125,000; *Magnificent Jewels, Geneva, November 15, 1995*

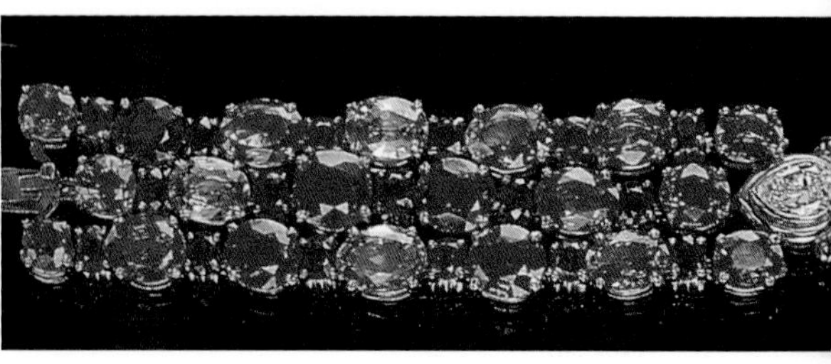

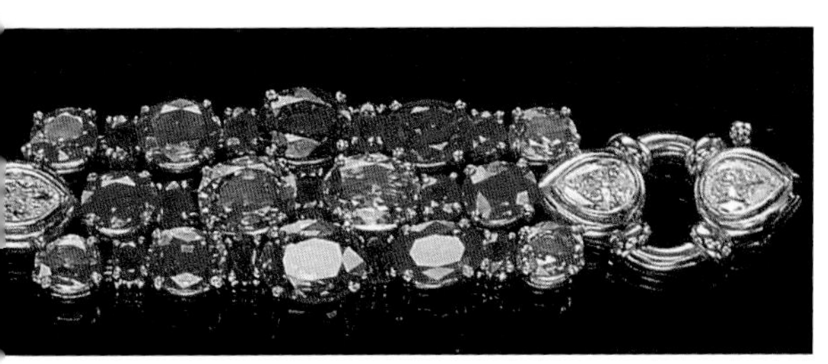

"The property of a gentleman," this exquisite suite comprises a necklace, bracelet, ear pendants, and a ring. The necklace, which is 46 cm long, features pavé-set diamonds and the front section has a scallop-edge. Each of the front segments is set with an oval-shaped sapphire and is spaced from the next by a baguette-cut diamond arrowhead connection. The graduated backchain is of pavé-set diamonds. The bracelet is 16.6 cm and is of a similar design, as are the ring and ear pendants.

Estimate: $10,000-12,000; Magnificent Jewels, Geneva, May 27, 1993

The sapphire and diamond suite of jewelry on the right was — in Christie's quaint terms — "the property of a lady." With its geometric design, it bears all the hallmarks of the Art Deco era and was produced by Cartier in around 1930. The focal point of the necklace is the central openwork buckle panel with its three sapphire drops. Meanwhile, the actual necklace is made from two rows of graduated rectangular-cut sapphires with square and baguette-cut diamond spacers attached to a back section of alternating sapphires and diamonds by diamond scroll connections. The two matching bracelets are set with a single line of graduated rectangular-cut sapphires and baguette-cut diamond two-stone spacers. Ear clips and a ring complete the suite.

Estimate: $75,000-105,000; *Important Jewellery, London, December 7, 1995*

This demi-suite of sapphire and diamond jewelry (right) consists of just a ring and a pair of ear clips. Made by Van Cleef & Arpels, the two pieces bear the company's innovative stamp: the invisibly set gemstone. The ring features a sapphire convex lozenge surrounded by a diamond collet cluster, which is set on pavé-set diamond shoulders and a platinum hoop. The ear clips are made in matching style.

Estimate: $25,000-33,000; *Magnificent Jewels, Geneva, May 18, 1995*

BROOCHES & BUCKLES

BROOCHES & BUCKLES

In ancient times, it was a pin. Now, it is a brooch. Over the years, they have been used to affix a whole variety of items including scarves, hats, and sleeves. In the last quarter of the 19th century, it was very fashionable for creatures from the insect, reptilian, and animal world to be reproduced in jewelry form. Some of the most popular brooches were of dragonflies, butterflies, bees, spiders, owls, swallows, frogs, and lizards. Often worn in multiples, they were used not only to secure pieces of clothing, but also as decoration on a woman's bodice.

This Victorian beetle brooch, mounted in silver and gold, has a pavé-set diamond body and wings with sapphire detail, as well as a ruby-set tail and eyes. It measures 3.7 cm wide.

Estimate: £1,500-2,000; *Important Jewellery, London, December 9, 1992*

This butterfly brooch was made circa 1870 with old mine-cut diamonds and cushion-shaped sapphires dotting its wings, body, and head.

Estimate: $6,400-8,500; *Magnificent Jewels, Geneva, May 19, 1994*

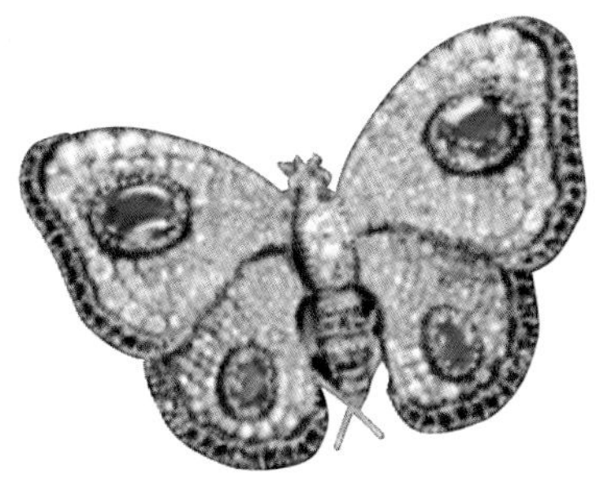

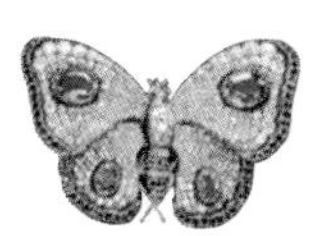

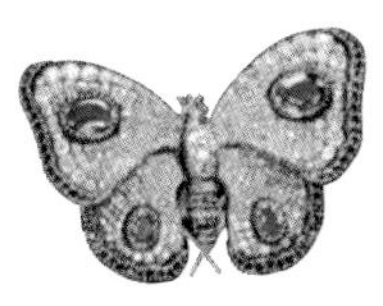

A matter of millimeters smaller than the one on the previous page, this Victorian gem-set moth brooch has diamond wings and a diamond body, an oval-shaped sapphire tail, and ruby eyes. It was made around 1880, when it was mounted in silver and gold.

Estimate: £2,500-3,000; *Important Jewellery London, June 21, 1995*

Although fairly modern, having been produced by Kutchinsky in 1967, this 18 carat gold rabbit brooch echoes the animal brooches of the last century. Set into the textured gold head and body are pear-shaped sapphire and pavé-set diamond eyes, a cabochon ruby nose, and diamond-set teeth. The firm of Kutchinsky, founded by Hirsch Kutchinsky and his son Morris, began manufacturing fine jewelry in East London in 1893. It was taken over by Morris's sons in 1930 and, after the war, was successful enough to open a store in London's Knightsbridge, where it remains today.

Estimate: $600-900/£400-600; *Jewellery Without Reserve, London, December 7, 1995*

The very cute pair of owls in this brooch have cabochon sapphire bodies, with ruby and diamond eyes. Designed by Cartier, it is 3.8 cm wide.

Estimate: £7,000-9,000; *Important Jewellery, London, December 13, 1989*

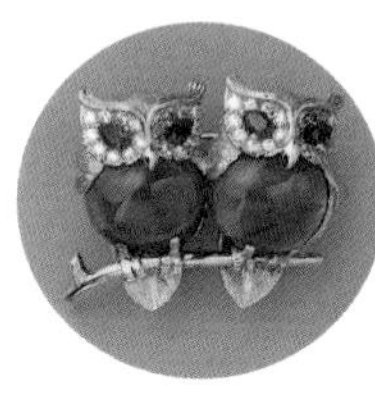

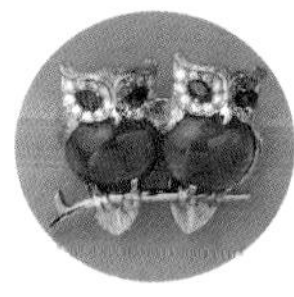

Another Cartier brooch, this time in the form of a cabochon and calibré-cut sapphire bird perched upon a rectangular-cut amethyst with diamond collet detail. Dating to around 1950, it measures 4 cm in height.

Estimate: £2,800-3,200; *Important Jewellery London, June 21, 1995*

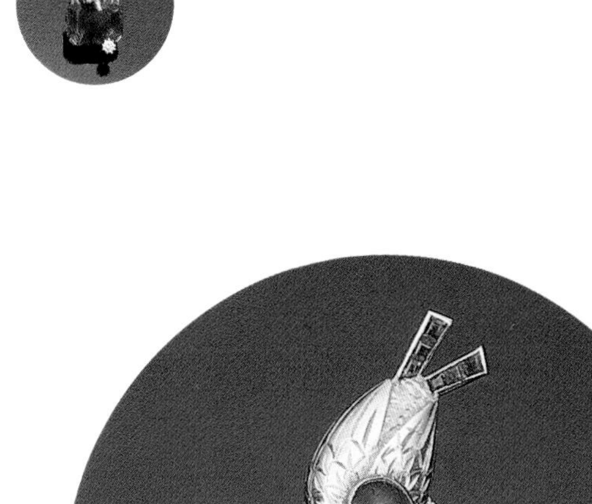

The centerpiece of this platinum-mounted Chantecler brooch is a rectangular-cut sapphire weighing approximately 7.46 carats; an accompanying certificate from the Gemmological Institute of America states that the stone changes color from dark blue to dark purple and blue under different circumstances. Surrounding the central gem is a circular and marquise-cut diamond and marquise-cut sapphire cluster frame. Pietro Capuano, a Neapolitan nobleman whose family had been in the antique jewelry trade in Capri immediately after the Second World War, founded Chantecler. He called the shop Chantecler because it was his nickname. Popular among high society, Chantecler was known for the originality and elegance of its jewelry.

Estimate: $18,000-22,000; *Magnificent Jewels, New York, October 24, 1995*

The oval-cut sapphire in this cluster brooch weighs 31.43 carats; the two-tiered surround is made from circular and marquise-cut diamonds. It was sold with a chain so that it could be used as a pendant, as it is in the photo.

Estimate:
$20,000-23,000;
Magnificent Jewels, Geneva, May 27, 1993

This beautifully elegant tassel brooch was created in around 1910 during the *Belle Epoque*, which means "Fine Period" in French. It refers to an era of settled and comfortable living that lasted from the end of the 19th century up until the outbreak of the First World War. This brooch is a fine example of the elaborate and sumptuous arts style that it produced.

In the center of the pear-shaped and old European-cut diamond bow mount is a cushion-shaped sapphire. Hanging below are three detachable sapphire collet and old European-cut diamond tassels.

Estimate: $13,500-16,500; *Magnificent Jewels, Geneva, November 15, 1995*

This exquisite sapphire and diamond flower clip brooch features Van Cleef & Arpels's trademark setting. Invisibly set sapphire petals are bordered by circular and pear-shaped diamonds, and surround a circular-cut diamond cluster representing the pistils. Mounted in platinum and 18 carat gold in about 1970, this brooch bears French assay marks.

Estimate: $60,000-80,000; *Magnificent Jewels, Geneva, November 20, 1997*

Another invisibly set flower brooch by Van Cleef & Arpels, this one from the estate of a Mrs J. P. Calsec. The sapphire petals, circular-cut diamond pistils, baguette-cut diamond stem, and pavé-set diamond leaves are all mounted in platinum.

Estimate: $22,000-27,000; *Magnificent Jewels, Geneva, May 18, 1995*

Van Cleef & Arpels produced this double clip brooch in 1935. While one flower has pavé-set diamond petals and a diamond cluster center, the other has calibré-cut sapphire petals and a diamond cluster center. The scrolled stem is made from baguette-cut diamonds. The mount is platinum and 18 carat gold.

Estimate: $17,000-21,000; *Magnificent Jewels, Geneva, May 18, 1995*

EARRINGS

EARRINGS

Earrings have been worn from earliest times, made from various kinds of metal and in a wide variety of styles. However, their popularity really soared during the Renaissance along with a trend for shorter hair. They have been worn ever since, by both men and women.

These magnificent Bulgari ear clips are set with a pair of cabochon sapphires weighing 44.97 and 45.17 carats; each surrounded by a pear-shaped diamond cluster. Accompanying certificates from the Gübelin Gemmological Laboratory state that the sapphires are from Kashmir and that the two represent a well-matched pair. Sets such as these are rare and exceptional. These extraordinary sapphires are thought to have been discovered in a valley in the

high Himalayas, above the virtually inaccessible village of Sunjam, in the Padar District of the state of Kashmir. The small upland valley is only 900 meters long and 365 meters wide, and is at an elevation of over 3,900 meters above sea level. They were probably mined sometime between 1883 and 1887, when the collection of sapphires was under the control of the Maharajah of Kashmir. Since that time, the recovery of stones of more than ten carats has been limited. From a technical point of view, the ear clips are a perfect combination of exceptional sapphires, great contrast with the diamond surround, elegance and restraint in the design of the mount, and, of course, distinctive Bulgari style.

Estimate: $700,000-800,000; *Magnificent Jewels, Geneva, May 27, 1993*

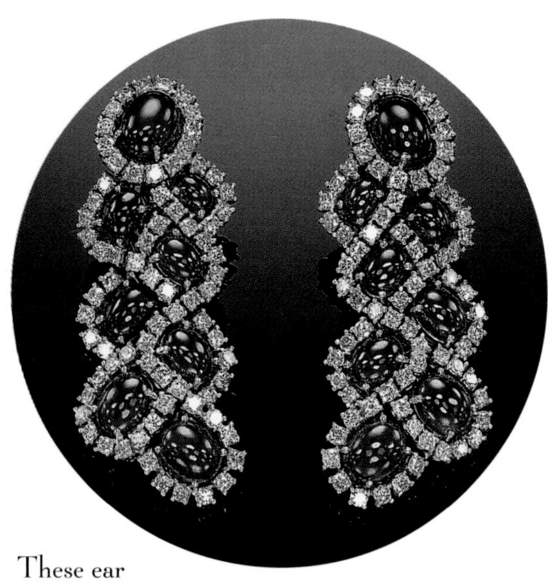

These ear pendants were designed to represent a cascade of cabochon sapphire and circular-cut diamond clusters. They are mounted in 18 carat white gold.

Estimate: $17,500-22,000; *Important Jewels, St Moritz, February 23/24, 1996*

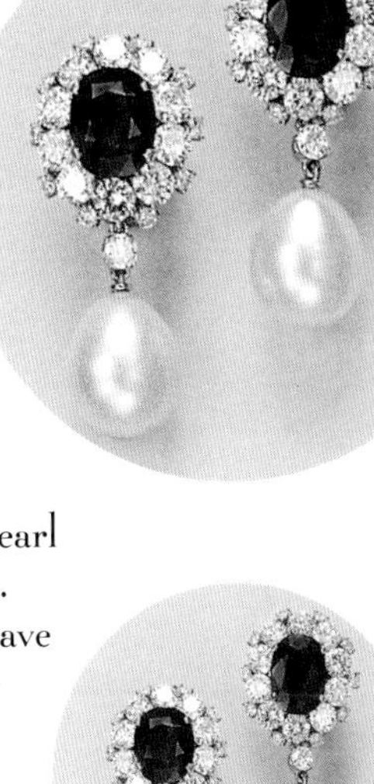

With this pair of earrings, each of the two cushion-shaped sapphire mounts, surrounded by a circular-cut diamond cluster, suspends a drop-shaped cultured pearl with diamond top. Cultured pearls have been very popular since the 1920s, because although they look very like natural pearls they are considerably less expensive.

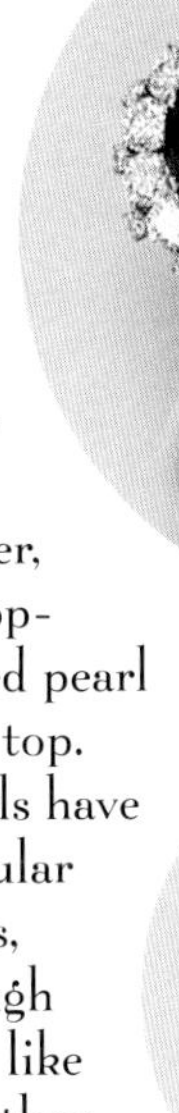

Estimate: $23,000-30,000; *Magnificent Jewels, Geneva, May 21, 1992*

Each of these ear pendants has a cushion-shaped sapphire and circular-cut diamond trefoil mount, which suspends a cascade of cushion-shaped sapphire and circular-cut diamond clusters.

Estimate: $13,000-16,000; *Magnificent Jewels, Geneva, May 27, 1993*

TIARAS

Tiara was the term used to describe the headdresses of the ancient Persians. More recently, tiaras have been worn by female members of royal or noble families on state or formal occasions. Tiaras come in many different shapes and sizes, some of which can also be worn as necklaces.

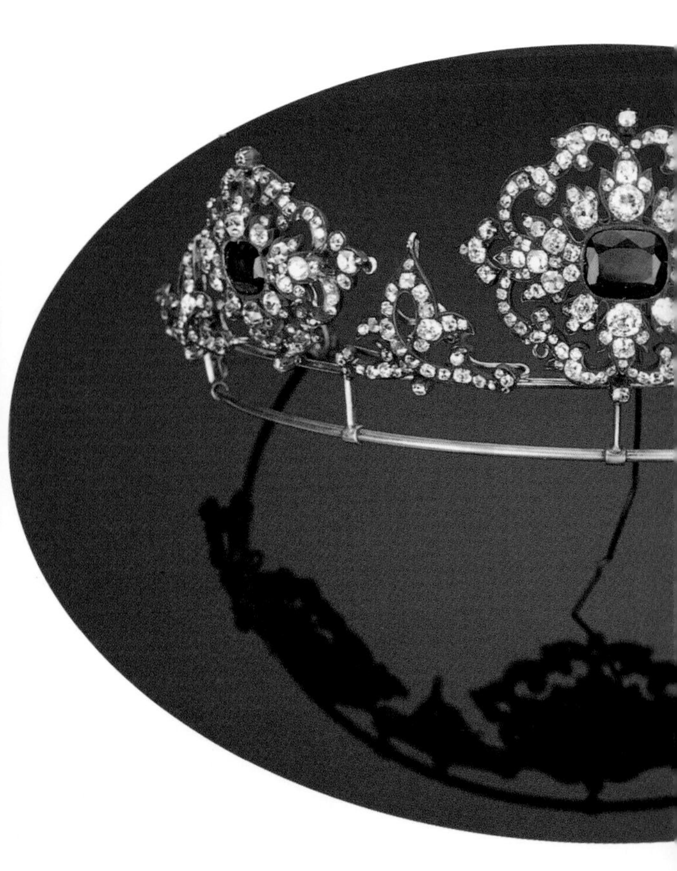

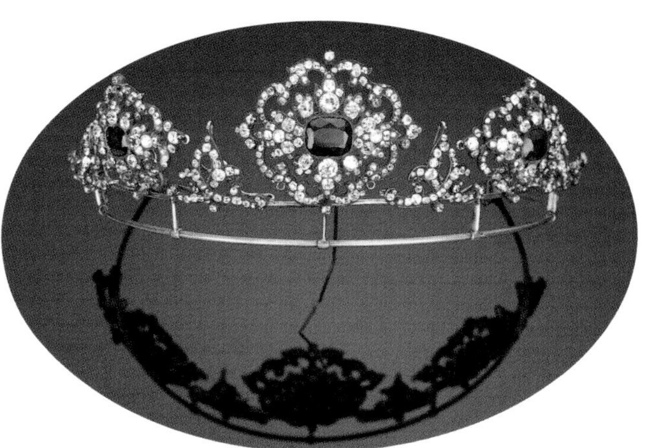

This antique tiara is encrusted with diamonds and synthetic sapphires — antique in Christie's terms means that the piece is over a century old. Believed to have been made around 1890, the tiara features a foliate and scroll design with three graduated penwork clusters that are set with cushion-shaped synthetic sapphires. The mount is made of gold and silver. The tiara actually breaks down into a necklace or bangle and brooch, for which there are attachments.

Estimate: £20,000-25,000/$32,000-39,000; *Christie's Antique Jewellery, Antique Jewels and Rings, London, October 9, 1996*

GEMSTONES

GEMSTONES

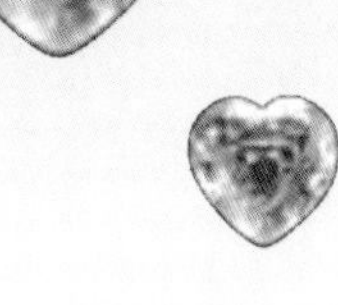

These 20 yellow sapphires, each one set with two heart-shaped pink sapphires, are accompanied by a design for a necklace.

Estimate: $10,000-12,500; *Magnificent Jewels, Geneva, May 18, 1995*

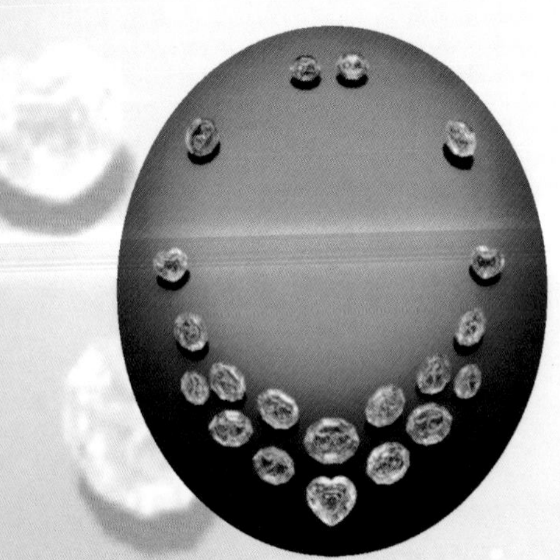

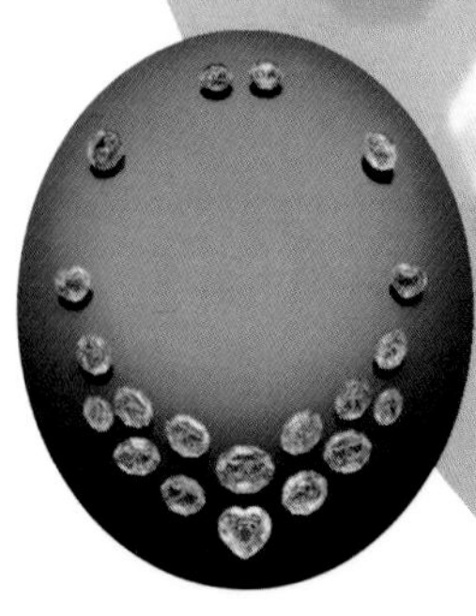

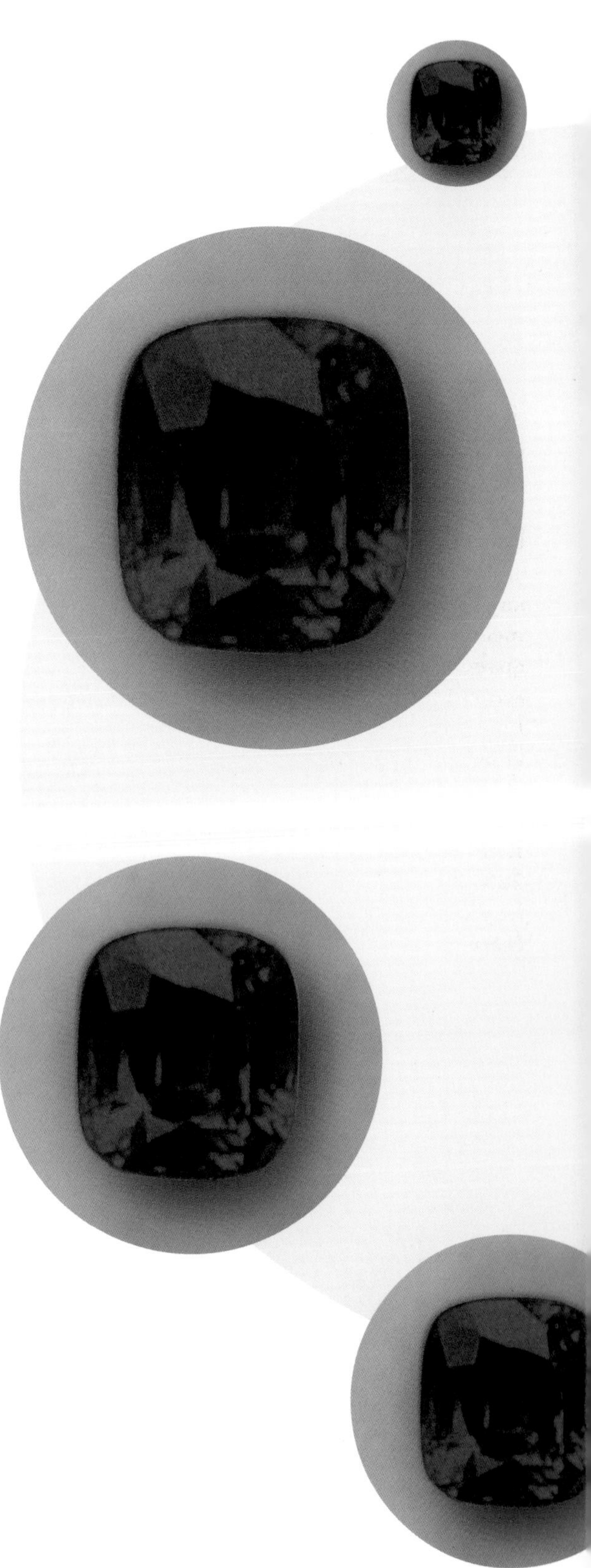

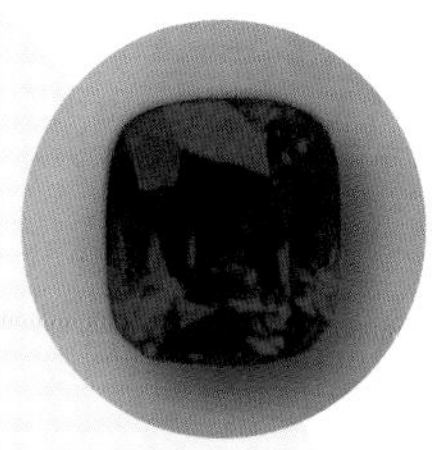

This fine unmounted, cushion-shaped sapphire, which weighs 58.46 carats shows a beautifully even color and no indication of any thermal treatment. This size and quality of the sapphire account for its price. However, little is known of the history of this stone

Estimate: $200,000-$250,000: *Important Jewels, St Moritz, February 23/24, 1996*

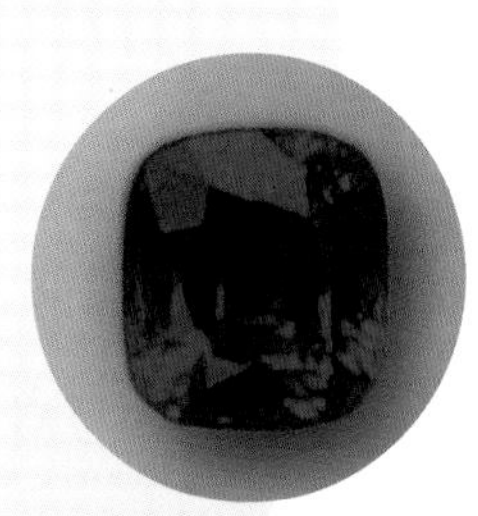

INDEX